GREATEST OF ALL TIME SPORTS STARS

THE GREATEST TRACK STARS OF ALL TIME

I0807563

Gareth Stevens PUBLISHING

BY MATTHEW JANKOWSKI

Please visit our website, www.garethstevens.com. For a free color catalog of all our high-quality books, call toll free 1-800-542-2595 or fax 1-877-542-2596.

Cataloging-in-Publication Data

Names: Jankowski, Matthew.
Title: The greatest track stars of all time / Matthew Jankowski.
Description: New York : Gareth Stevens Publishing, 2020. | Series: Greatest of all time: sports stars | Includes glossary and index.
Identifiers: ISBN 9781538247877(pbk.) | ISBN 9781538247891(library bound) | ISBN 9781538247884(6 pack)
Subjects: LCSH: Track and field athletes–Rating of–Juvenile literature. | Track and field athletes–Statistics–Juvenile literature. | Track and field athletes–Biography–Juvenile literature. | Track and field–Records–Juvenile literature. | Track and field–History–Juvenile literature.
Classification: LCC GV1060.55 J36 2019 | DDC 796.420922 B–dc23

First Edition

Published in 2020 by
Gareth Stevens Publishing
111 East 14th Street, Suite 349
New York, NY 10003

Copyright © 2020 Gareth Stevens Publishing

Designer: Katelyn E. Reynolds
Editor: Emily Mahoney

Photo credits: Cover, p. 1 T Marshall - British Athletics/British Athletics via Getty Images; cover, pp. 1–32 (series art) Dmitry Kostrov/Shutterstock.com; cover, pp. 1–32 (series background) rangizzz/Shutterstock.com; pp. 5, 29 (shoe graphic) In-Finity/Shutterstock.com; p. 6 CARL DE SOUZA/AFP/Getty Images; p. 7 Ian Walton/Getty Images; pp. 8, 14 Tony Duffy/Allsport/Getty Images; p. 9 Matthias Hangst/Getty Images; p. 10 Central Press/Getty Images; p. 11 Photo12/UIG/Getty Images; p. 13, 15 David Madison/Getty Images; p. 17 HASLIN Frederic/Corbis via Getty Images; p. 19 Bettmann/Getty Images; p. 21 photocosmos1/Shutterstock.com; p. 22 GABRIEL BOUYS/AFP/Getty Images; p. 23 Pascal Rondeau/Allsport/Getty Images; p. 24 thelefty/Shutterstock.com; p. 25 Gilbert Iundt/Corbis/VCG via Getty Images; p. 26 Simon Bruty/Allsport/Getty Images; p. 27 Tony Duffy/Getty Images.

All rights reserved. No part of this book may be reproduced in any form without permission in writing from the publisher, except by a reviewer.

Printed in the United States of America

CPSIA compliance information: Batch #CW20GS: For further information contact Gareth Stevens, New York, New York at 1-800-542-2595.

CONTENTS

WORDS IN THE GLOSSARY APPEAR IN **BOLD** TEXT THE FIRST TIME THEY ARE USED IN THE TEXT.

ON YOUR MARK, GET SET, GO!

Lace up your running shoes and take the starting line! Track and field events contain some of the oldest sports in history. In ancient Greece, all the way back in 776 BC, athletes competed against each other in the Olympic Games to see who could run fastest, jump highest, and throw farthest.

In this book, you will learn about the greatest modern athletes in these sporting events. In reading about their accomplishments and learning their stories, you might be **inspired** to get out and try to become the next great track and field athlete!

TRACK AND FIELD EVENTS

RUNNING EVENTS	100M DASH, 200M DASH, 400M, 800M, 1500M, THE MILE, 3000M, 5000M
JUMPING EVENTS	LONG JUMP, HIGH JUMP, TRIPLE JUMP, POLE VAULT
HURDLES	55M, 100M, 110M, 400M
THROWING EVENTS	DISCUS, JAVELIN, SHOT PUT, HAMMER THROW
RELAYS	4x100M, 4x200M, 4x400M, 4x800M

THERE IS A TRACK AND FIELD EVENT FOR EVERYONE TO **EXCEL** IN WITH OVER 20 EVENTS ACROSS FIVE DIFFERENT GROUPS! ALL DISTANCES HERE ARE LISTED IN METERS (M).

MEETING AND COMPETING ALL THE TIME

THE OLYMPIC GAMES ARE PROBABLY THE MOST WIDELY KNOWN TRACK AND FIELD COMPETITION, BUT THERE ARE MANY MORE. COMPETITIONS IN TRACK ARE CALLED MEETS AND CAN BE HELD BOTH INDOORS AND OUTDOORS. THE MOST POPULAR PROFESSIONAL MEETS ARE THE NATIONAL MASTERS CHAMPIONSHIP EVENTS FOR AMERICAN ATHLETES AND THE WORLD MASTERS CHAMPIONSHIP EVENTS FOR ATHLETES FROM AROUND THE WORLD.

USAIN BOLT

Sprinting events involve some of the fastest athletes in all sports, and Usain Bolt was certainly an electric athlete! Arguably the fastest man in the world during his peak, Bolt set a world record for the 100-meter race, running it in 9.58 seconds, and the 200-meter event, with a time of 19.19 seconds.

Born in Jamaica, Bolt attended the 2008 Olympic Games to compete against the world's fastest men. He became the first man in Olympic history to win both the 100- and 200-meter races. He returned in 2012 and 2016, defending his title as **reigning** champion. Bolt won nine Olympic gold medals before choosing to go out on top when he retired in 2017.

SOME ATHLETES ARE KNOWN FOR TAKING A VICTORY LAP AFTER WINNING A RACE. USAIN BOLT IS KNOWN FOR STRIKING HIS **ICONIC** "LIGHTNING BOLT" POSE.

HOW FAST DID BOLT TRAVEL?

USAIN BOLT SET HIS WORLD RECORD OF 9.58 SECONDS IN THE 100-METER EVENT AT THE BERLIN 2009 TRACK AND FIELD WORLD CHAMPIONSHIPS. IT HAS BEEN MEASURED THAT BOLT HIT A TOP SPEED OF 27.8 MPH DURING THAT RACE, WHICH IS DOCUMENTED AS THE FASTEST-EVER HUMAN FOOTSPEED.

FLORENCE "FLO JO" GRIFFITH JOYNER

The flip side to the fastest human category is American sprinter Florence Griffith Joyner. Known best by her nickname, Flo Jo, she set world records for women in the 100-meter dash at 10.49 seconds and the 200 meters at 21.23 seconds. Even more impressive is that she set these records in 1988. Her records have stood for over 30 years!

At the Olympics in Seoul, Korea, in 1988, Flo Jo won three gold medals in the 100-meter, 200-meter and 4x100 meter relay. The world watched stunned when she broke a 9-year-old world record in a qualifying **heat** and then broke her own record during the final!

FLO JO ACCOMPLISHED HER GOAL OF BEING THE FASTEST WOMAN IN THE WORLD! SADLY, SHE DIED AT ONLY 38 YEARS OLD.

IN 2005, ALLYSON FELIX WENT UNDEFEATED IN THE 200M, WINNING THE WORLD TITLE AND RECORDING THE THREE FASTEST TIMES IN THE WORLD.

ALLYSON FELIX

ANOTHER GREAT TRACK ATHLETE, ALLYSON FELIX, WON NINE OLYMPIC MEDALS IN EVENTS SUCH AS THE 200 METERS AND THE 400 METERS. SHE BECAME THE FIRST ATHLETE SINCE FLO JO TO WIN THREE GOLD MEDALS IN A SINGLE OLYMPICS IN THE 2012 LONDON GAMES. SHE WON HER FIRST OLYMPIC MEDAL AT AGE 18!

JESSE OWENS

Sometimes athletes are great both because of what they do on the track, and what they do off of it. Jesse Owens certainly managed greatness both ways! On the track, Jesse was one of the fastest runners of his time. In 1935, he managed to set three world records and tie another one, all within 45 minutes!

Just as impressive as his athletic accomplishments was the way that Jesse Owens lived his life. After retiring from running on the track, Jesse devoted his life to working with **underprivileged** kids. He traveled as an inspirational speaker, passing on his message that anyone is capable of doing anything!

JESSE OWENS PASSED AWAY IN 1980. HERE HE IS RACING IN THE FINAL OF THE 100 METERS AT THE 1936 OLYMPICS IN BERLIN, GERMANY.

RACING PAST RACISM

ADOLPH HITLER AND HIS RACIST NAZI PARTY WERE RULING GERMANY DURING THE 1936 OLYMPICS. THEY BELIEVED THAT WHITE-SKINNED PEOPLE WERE BETTER THAN ANYONE ELSE. OWENS BECAME THE FIRST ATHLETE TO WIN FOUR GOLD MEDALS IN A SINGLE OLYMPICS, PROVING THAT THE COLOR OF ONE'S SKIN DOESN'T HAVE ANYTHING TO DO WITH INDIVIDUAL EXCELLENCE.

GAIL DEVERS

Gail Devers achieved greatness in a track and field event known as the hurdles. In these races, runners have to keep stride to the finish line as they leap over **obstacles** placed in their way. Gail Devers is arguably the fastest female combination sprinter and hurdler in track history.

Gail stood at the top of the **podium** at both the 1992 and 1996 Olympic Games, winning gold in the 100-meter dash. She also holds the American women's record for fastest time in the 100-meter hurdles at 12.33 seconds. She set this record in 2000 and, as of 2019, it has yet to be broken.

GAIL DEVERS SHARED A LOOK OF DETERMINATION CARRIED BY MANY TRACK ATHLETES. GAIL DEVERS WAS KNOWN FOR HER LONG FINGERNAILS, USUALLY PAINTED BLUE!

HURDLING EVERY OBSTACLE

FOR TWO YEARS AFTER THE 1988 OLYMPIC GAMES, GAIL FELT TIRED AND UNLIKE HERSELF. FINALLY, SHE WAS DIAGNOSED WITH AN ILLNESS CALLED GRAVES' DISEASE. HER FEET GOT SO SWOLLEN THAT THEY ALMOST HAD TO BE **AMPUTATED**. GAIL'S INCREDIBLE RESOLVE PUSHED HER THROUGH TREATMENT TO RETURN TO RACING, WINNING GOLD IN 1992 AND 1996.

CARL LEWIS

Carl Lewis is another legendary sprinter. People talk about "decorated" Olympians, or competitors who have won multiple medals. That certainly describes Carl! In fact, he has a staggering 10 Olympic medals, nine gold and one silver.

From 1976 to 1996, Carl Lewis dominated the 100-meter, 200-meter, and long jump. He won four gold medals in a single Olympics, achieving victory in every event he was in. Carl wasn't just the fastest runner. He also used his speed to succeed at the long jump in four Olympic Games in a row!

CARL LEWIS RAN THE ANCHOR LEG OF THEN MEN'S 4X100 METER RELAY IN THE 1992 OLYMPICS. THE ANCHOR IS THE LAST PERSON TO RUN FOR EACH TEAM IN THE RELAY, COMMONLY BECAUSE THEY'RE THE FASTEST.

THE LONGEST JUMP?

WHILE CARL LEWIS DID WIN GOLD MEDALS IN THE LONG JUMP, HE'S NOT THE WORLD RECORD HOLDER. MIKE POWELL HAS HIM BEAT, JUMPING 8.95 METERS, OR 29 FEET AND 4.25 INCHES, IN 1991. AS OF 2019, THE WOMEN'S LONG JUMP RECORD IS 7.52 METERS, OR 24 FEET AND 8 INCHES, SET BY GALINA CHRISTYAKOVA IN 1988.

MICHAEL JOHNSON

Welcome to the middle-distance events, which are the 200 meters and 400 meters. Welcome, and good luck outrunning Michael Johnson! In the 1990s, Michael was briefly called the World's Fastest Man. He set world records in the 200 meters at 19.32 seconds and in the 400 meters at 43.18 seconds.

While these records have since been broken, Michael Johnson still has one world record to his name as of 2019, setting it as a member of the 4x400 meter relay team. Altogether, he blazed his way to four Olympic gold medals and eight track and field world championship gold medals before he retired.

MICHAEL JOHNSON WAS KNOWN FOR HIS **TENACITY** ON THE TRACK. MICHAEL HAD LONG LEGS, WHICH HELPED HIM TO TAKE LARGE STRIDES AND OUTRUN THE COMPETITION!

PASSING THE TORCH

MICHAEL JOHNSON STILL HELD THE WORLD RECORD IN THE 400 METERS UNTIL 2016. WAYDE VAN NIEKERK FROM SOUTH AFRICA BEAT MICHAEL JOHNSON'S RECORD WITH A **BLISTERING** TIME OF 43.03 SECONDS. WAYDE VAN NIEKERK IS STILL COMPETING TODAY! WILL HE BREAK HIS OWN RECORD SOMEDAY?

PAAVO NURMI

All the way back in the 1920s, Paavo Nurmi, who was from Finland, started winning every race. For the Olympic mile, 5,000 meters, and 10,000 meters, and basically every long-distance event, it was Nurmi first across the finish line. His success earned him the nickname the "Flying Finn."

The Flying Finn certainly knew how to run! At the time, Nurmi held world records in the mile, 5,000 meter, and 10,000 meters. These have since been broken, but in the 1920s, Nurmi was untouchable. He is the only runner other than Carl Lewis to win nine Olympic gold medals.

PAAVO NURMI WAS CALLED THE "WONDER MAN OF THE 1924 OLYMPICS" BECAUSE HE DID SO WELL. HERE HE IS WINNING THE 5,000-METER RACE.

RUNNING WITH ENDURANCE

ENDURANCE, OR THE ABILITY TO DO SOMETHING FOR A LONG TIME, IS A KEY WORD FOR LONG DISTANCE RUNNERS. AND PAAVO NURMI WAS A MASTER OF ENDURANCE. HE CARRIED A STOPWATCH TO KEEP TRACK OF TIME RUNNING. PAAVO BELIEVED IT WAS BETTER TO RUN AGAINST TIME INSTEAD OF HIS COMPETITION TO KEEP GETTING FASTER EACH RACE.

ELIUD KIPCHOGE

The marathon is a 26.2 mile (42.2 km) run. It's a feat of strength and will for the average person just to finish. For marathon runners, it becomes another race against the clock. The Olympic marathon usually doesn't get the same attention as events like the 100 meter sprint, but it ranks as one of the most impressive running events. And in 2016, the winner was the great Eliud Kipchoge.

From the African country of Kenya, Eliud Kipchoge broke the record for the fastest marathon ever in 2018. He ran the Berlin Marathon in 2 hours, 1 minute and 39 seconds. Kipchoge is still running today! How fast will he run the marathon next?

WHEN ELIUD KIPCHOGE BROKE THE TAPE OF THE 2017 BERLIN MARATHON, HE CROSSED THE FINISH LINE WITH HIS HANDS UP LIKE HE WASN'T EVEN TIRED!

COULD THE FUTURE BE NOW?

ELIUD HAS STATED PLANS TO TRY TO RUN A MARATHON IN LESS THAN 2 HOURS SOON! RESEARCHERS ARE PREDICTING BASED ON DATA TRENDS THAT A MARATHON IN LESS THAN 2 HOURS WON'T HAPPEN UNTIL 2032. LET'S SEE IF ELIUD CAN MAKE THIS INCREDIBLE ACCOMPLISHMENT AND PROVE THEM WRONG!

HIGH JUMP GREATS

Track and field is about more than just running fast. There are many other events that are not foot races. The high jump is an exciting example. For women, nobody has dominated the high jump like Stefka Kostadinova, who has the current world record for highest jump at 2.09 meters.

For men, the athlete to beat is Javier Sotomayor. He holds the world record highest jump at 2.45 meters. Javier has **humorously** said that he was afraid of heights when he was 10 years old. He said that by practicing and talking to his coach, he got over his fear little by little to become the greatest high jumper of all time.

JAVIER SOTOMAYOR

MOST HIGH JUMPERS DO THE "FOSBURY FLOP" JUMP TECHNIQUE NAMED AFTER AMERICAN ATHLETE DICK FOSBURY WHERE A JUMPER'S BACK ARCHES UP AND OVER THE HIGH BAR.

STEFKA KOSTADINOVA

GOING FOR THE GOLD

BOTH STEFKA KOSTADINOVA AND JAVIER SOTOMAYOR HAVE WON OLYMPIC GOLD. STEFKA WON DURING THE 1996 OLYMPICS, AND SHE ALSO HAS FIVE GOLD MEDALS FROM THE WORLD INDOOR CHAMPIONSHIPS ACROSS HER CAREER. JAVIER WON CUBA ITS FIRST-EVER OLYMPIC HIGH JUMP MEDAL IN 1992, BRINGING HONOR TO HIS HOME COUNTRY.

POLE VAULT STARS

From the high jump, we move to the highest-flying event, the pole vault! Probably the most famous pole vaulter is Sergey Bubka, who comes from Ukraine. Bubka started pole vaulting when he was nine years old and kept soaring higher and higher. His world record of 6.14 meters is the highest-ever pole vault.

The most elevated woman in track and field is Yelena Isinbayeva from Russia. Right up there with Bubka, she has the current women's world record vault of 5.06 meters. She achieved this only one year after winning the gold medal at the 2008 Olympic Games in Beijing, China.

HERE IS AN ACTION SHOT OF YELENA ISINBAYEVA RIGHT BEFORE SHE USES THE POLE TO VAULT HERSELF UP AND OVER TO COMPLETE HER JUMP.

SERGEY BUBKA CAN BE SEEN HERE COMPETING IN THE 1992 SUMMER OLYMPICS IN BARCELONA, SPAIN.

POLE VAULT HISTORY

IN POLE VAULTING, AN ATHLETE USES A LONG FLEXIBLE POLE TO PROPEL UP AND OVER A BAR THAT IS PROPPED VERY HIGH IN THE AIR. THE FIRST PEOPLE TO POLE VAULT CAME FROM EUROPE, WHERE MEN USED POLES TO CROSS CANALS FILLED WITH WATER. YOU CAN SEARCH "HOW TO POLE VAULT" ONLINE TO SEE DIFFERENT TECHNIQUES THAT POLE VAULTERS USE.

EXTRAORDINARY THROWERS

For these two athletes, it's not about how fast you can run or how high you can jump, but how far you can throw. Natalya Lisovskaya launched the world record shot put throw at 22.63 meters. She set this record all the way back in 1987, and it has yet to be broken!

Jan Zelezny is the greatest men's javelin thrower of all time. Zelezny is known for claiming six world records based on different types of spears he threw during events. He won gold at three different Olympic Games and is a three-time World Champion. His javelin throw of 98.48 meters is the farthest in history.

JAN ZELEZNY

NATALYA LISOVSKAYA IS THROWING SHOT PUT HERE IN 1985. THE BALL THAT SHE IS HOLDING IS CALLED A "SHOT."

EVERYTHING BEING THROWN AROUND

THERE ARE TWO MORE THROWING EVENTS IN TRACK AND FIELD: THE DISCUS AND THE HAMMER THROW. IN THE DISCUS, ATHLETES SPIN AROUND MULTIPLE TIMES BEFORE LAUNCHING A HEAVY METAL DISC AS FAR AS THEY CAN. FOR THE HAMMER THROW, GOOD ADVICE IS TO HOLD ON TIGHT AS ATHLETES HURL A BALL AND CHAIN. ATHLETES NEED TO BE VERY STRONG TO EXCEL AT THESE EVENTS.

CROSSING THE FINISH LINE

These men and women are the fastest-running, farthest-jumping, highest-flying, and strongest-throwing track and field athletes of all time! From all across the world, these athletes have competed in world championships and in Olympic Games to bring home victory. Many of them shattered records and set the new times and distances to beat!

This is the end of this book, but the story continues with you! Put on your running shoes or pick up a discus and get on out there! Set and break your own records, and race and compete against your friends. Every track athlete knows that getting faster and stronger takes practice and hard work. The track awaits!

THREE ACCOMPLISHED TRACK AND FIELD ATHLETES WITH DISABILITIES

ATHLETE	EVENT	WHAT MAKES THEM GREAT?
TIM HARRIS	MULTIPLE EVENTS	TIM WAS CAPTAIN OF HIS SPECIAL OLYMPICS BASKETBALL TEAM. HE CURRENTLY OWNS HIS OWN RESTAURANT AND DONATES MONEY TO SUPPORT THE SPECIAL OLYMPICS.
LORETTA CLAIBORNE	THE MILE, THE HALF MARATHON	DESPITE BEING BORN PARTIALLY BLIND AND UNABLE TO WALK OR TALK UNTIL SHE WAS 4, LORETTA HAS PLACED IN THE TOP 100 FEMALE FINISHERS OF THE BOSTON MARATHON!
ANDREW PETERSON	1,500 METERS, 3,000 METERS AND 5,000 METERS	ANDREW WAS BORN WITH DISABILITIES, BUT THIS DIDN'T STOP HIM FROM WINNING THREE GOLD MEDALS AT THE 2014 SPECIAL OLYMPICS!

ALL PEOPLE CAN COMPETE AND ACHIEVE SUCCESS IN TRACK AND FIELD. EVERY 4 YEARS, THE SUMMER SPECIAL OLYMPICS SEES ATHLETES WITH DISABILITIES PUSH THEMSELVES TO THE LIMITS OF THE HUMAN BODY!

THE SPECIAL OLYMPICS

THE SPECIAL OLYMPICS IS AN ORGANIZATION FORMED IN 1968 THAT ALLOWS ATHLETES WITH PHYSICAL AND INTELLECTUAL DISABILITIES TO COMPLETE AGAINST EACH OTHER. EVENTS AT THE SPECIAL OLYMPICS MAY BE MODIFIED, OR CHANGED, SO THAT PEOPLE IN WHEELCHAIRS OR WITH OTHER DISABILITIES CAN COMPETE AGAINST EACH OTHER AND HAVE FUN!

GLOSSARY

amputate: to remove a body part through surgery

blistering: very harsh or powerful

electrify: to cause someone to feel great excitement

excel: to be or do better than others

heat: one of several races that are held in order to decide who will be in a final race

humorous: something funny

iconic: a person who is very successful and admired

inspire: to cause someone to want to do something

obstacle: something that makes it difficult to do something

podium: a raised platform for a speaker or performer

reign: the period of time during which someone is the best or the most important

tenacity: very determined to do something

underprivileged: having fewer advantages, privileges, and opportunities than most people

FOR MORE INFORMATION

BOOKS

Buckley Jr., James. *Who Was Jesse Owens?* New York, NY: Penguin Workshop, 2015.

My Running Journal: Run Log Notebook. Scotts Valley, CA: Createspace Independent Publishing Platform, 2015.

Reynolds, Jason. *Ghost.* New York, NY: Atheneum Books, 2016.

WEBSITES

USA Track and Field—Youth Athletes
www.usatf.org/Youth.aspx
This USA track and field website for kids features athlete bios, time statistics, and a calendar of upcoming events for kids to watch or participate in!

Kids Sports—Track and Field
www.allstaractivities.com/sports/trackandfield/track.htm
This informative website contains information about track equipment, terminology, and tips for kids' first meets!

Track and Field Running Events
www.ducksters.com/sports/trackandfieldrunning.php
A fun website that has informative sections about track events and athletes, as well as some sports-related games.

Publisher's note to educators and parents: Our editors have carefully reviewed these websites to ensure that they are suitable for students. Many websites change frequently, however, and we cannot guarantee that a site's future contents will continue to meet our high standards of quality and educational value. Be advised that students should be closely supervised whenever they access the Internet.

INDEX